GIFTED & TALENTED®

To develop
your child's gifts
and talents

DICTIONARY

A Reference Workbook for Ages 6-8

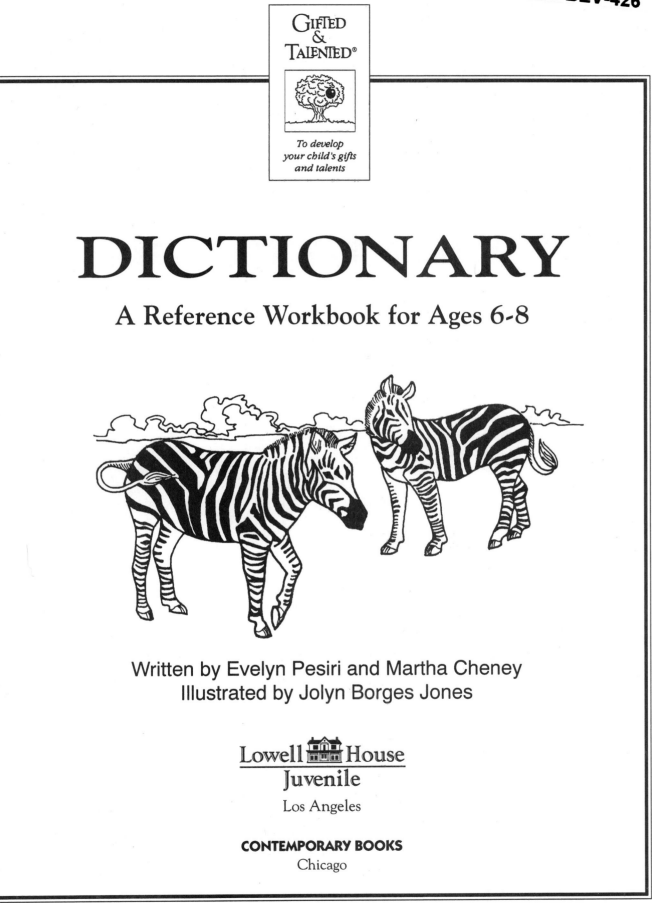

Written by Evelyn Pesiri and Martha Cheney
Illustrated by Jolyn Borges Jones

Lowell House
Juvenile

Los Angeles

CONTEMPORARY BOOKS

Chicago

LEGEND

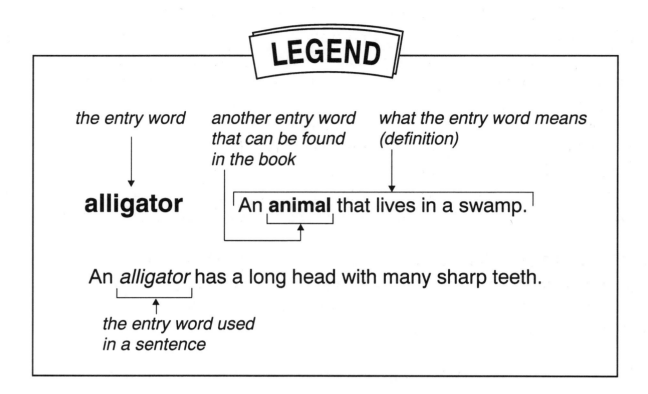

the entry word

another entry word that can be found in the book

what the entry word means (definition)

alligator

An **animal** that lives in a swamp.

An *alligator* has a long head with many sharp teeth.

the entry word used in a sentence

Manufactured in the United States of America

ISBN 1-56565-183-9

10 9 8 7 6 5 4 3 2 1

Lowell House books can be purchased at special discounts when ordered in bulk for premiums and special sales. Contact Department VH at the following address:
Lowell House Juvenile
2029 Century Park East
Suite 3290
Los Angeles, CA 90067

GIFTED & TALENTED® REFERENCE WORKBOOKS will help develop your child's natural talents and gifts by providing questions and pencil activities to enhance critical and creative thinking skills. These skills of logic and reasoning teach children **how** to think. They are precisely the skills emphasized by teachers of gifted and talented children.

Thinking skills are the skills needed to be able to learn anything at any time. If a child has a grasp of how to think, school success and even success in life will become more assured. In addition, the child will become self-confident as he or she approaches new tasks with the ability to think them through and discover solutions.

GIFTED & TALENTED® REFERENCE WORKBOOKS present these skills in a unique way, combining the basic subject areas of reading, language arts, and math with dictionary skills, map skills, and other reference-book skills. Here are some of the thinking skills you will find:

- Deduction — the ability to reach a logical conclusion by interpreting clues

- Understanding Relationships — the ability to recognize how objects, shapes, and words are similar or dissimilar; to classify and categorize

- Sequencing — the ability to organize events, numbers; to recognize patterns

- Inference — the ability to reach logical conclusions from given or assumed evidence

- Creative Thinking — the ability to generate unique ideas; to compare and contrast the same elements in different situations; to present imaginative solutions to problems

How to Use GIFTED & TALENTED® REFERENCE WORKBOOKS:

Each book contains thinking activities that challenge children. You may need to work with your child on many of the pages, especially with the child who is a nonreader. However, even a nonreader can master thinking skills, and the sooner your child learns how to think, the better. Read the books with your child and, if necessary, explain the activities. Let your child choose to answer the questions or do the activities that interest him or her. When interest wanes, stop. A page or two at a time may be enough, as the child should have fun while learning.

It is important to remember that these activities are designed to teach your child **how to think,** not how to find the right answer. Teachers of gifted children are never surprised when a child discovers a new "right" answer. For example, a child may be asked to choose the object that doesn't belong in this group: a table, a chair, a book, a desk. The best answer is **book,** since all the others are furniture. But a child could respond that all of them belong because they all could be found in an office or a library. The best way to react to this type of response is to praise the child and gently point out that there is another answer, too. While creativity should be encouraged, your child must look for the best and most **suitable** answer.

GIFTED AND TALENTED® REFERENCE WORKBOOKS have been written by teachers. Educationally sound and endorsed by a leader in the gifted field, this series will benefit any child who demonstrates curiosity, imagination, a sense of fun and wonder about the world, and a desire to learn. These books will open your child's mind to new experiences and help fulfill his or her true potential.

airplane A **vehicle** that flies in the sky. You can ride in an *airplane* to places that are very far away. Some airplanes are called jets. They go very fast!

alligator An **animal** that lives in a swamp. An *alligator* has a long head with many sharp teeth. It also has a long tail. Stay away from alligators—they can be dangerous!

alphabet All of the **letters** from A to Z. You can use the letters of the *alphabet* to spell words. There are 26 letters in the alphabet. Can you name them all? A, B, C, D . . .

What kind of animal is this?

animal Any living thing that can move from place to place. *Animals* can get **food** for themselves and can see and hear. A **bird,** an **insect,** a **whale,** a **snake,** a **fish,** a **frog,** and a person are all animals.

ant A small **insect** that lives with other *ants* in a large family called a colony. Watch out for ants at your next picnic!

apple A fruit that grows on a **tree**. *Apples* come in many colors, like red, green, and yellow. All apples are delicious—and good for you, too!

Which color is this apple?

artist   A person who is good at making or doing special things. Some *artists* make **pictures** or statues. Some artists dance, and other artists make music. What kind of artist are you?

bag   A **container** that can be made of paper, cloth, plastic, or leather. You can put things in a *bag* to keep them together or to carry them. Some bags have handles to hold.

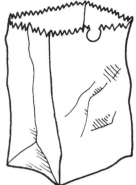

What do you think is inside this bag?

banana   A fruit that grows on a **tree**. Most *bananas* are yellow when they are ready to eat. A banana has a strong skin that protects it. You have to peel off the skin before you eat a banana. Do you peel off the skin of any other fruits before you eat them?

bear   A large, strong, furry **animal** with sharp claws. *Bears* are wild and live in the **forest**. They are fun to watch, but don't get too close! Bears can attack people.

bed   A place to sleep that is soft and warm. A *bed* can be a piece of furniture or a pile of hay. What kind of bed do you have? What kind of bed does a baby **bird** have?

bee   A flying **insect**. A *bee* has a hairy **body,** four wings, and a stinger. If a bee is afraid of you, it might sting you. When it's flying, a bee's wings make a buzzing sound.

bicycle A **vehicle** that you can ride that has two **wheels**. To ride a *bicycle,* you push the pedals to make the wheels move. You can turn the handlebars to go around a **corner** or to move from left to right. Do you know how to ride a bicycle?

bird An **animal** that has feathers and a hard beak, or mouth. All *birds* have wings, and most birds can fly. Some birds like to build their **nests** high in the **trees**. Birds can talk to each other, but they don't use words like people do. What kinds of sounds do birds make?

birthday The day you were born. Your *birthday* comes once every year. Every time you have a birthday, you add one more year to your age. How old are you now? How many birthdays have you had?

*Which is not an **animal**? Be careful!*
*Look up **animal** to help you decide.*
Are you an animal?

boat   A **vehicle** that floats in **water**. A *boat* can carry people or cargo across a **lake** or an **ocean**. Some boats have a motor to help them move. But other boats have sails to catch the wind.

head

toes

body   All of you, from the top of your head all the way down to the tips of your toes. Your *body* has lots of parts, like your lips and your legs, your nose and your knees. Can you name some other parts of your body?

book   A group of paper pages between two covers. Some *books* have words and no **pictures,** and other books have both words *and* pictures! This dictionary is a book. Does it have pictures? Does it have words?

Can you tell a story from this book?

boot   A high **shoe** that covers your ankle. You can wear rubber *boots* in the **rain** so your feet don't get wet. Why else would you wear boots?

bottle   A **container** that is used to hold **liquids** or **foods**. A *bottle* can be made of **glass** or plastic. Bottles can hold **juice, water,** perfume, or soap. A bottle can also hold ketchup or mustard.

bowl   A deep, round **plate** that has sides. You use a *bowl* to hold **foods** like rice, cereal, or soup. What else can you put in a bowl?

What do you think is inside this bowl?

box   A **container** that is made out of wood, plastic, metal, or folded cardboard. On your **birthday,** your **friend** might give you a *box* that is all wrapped up and tied with a bow.

What is inside this box?

boy   A male child. When a *boy* grows up, he is called a man. Are you a boy?

brush   A **tool** with bristles and a handle. You can use a *brush* to put **paint** on the **wall** or to paint a **picture**. You use a brush to clean your teeth or to smooth your hair. You can even sweep the floor with a brush that has a long handle.

Do you know what this kind of brush is called?

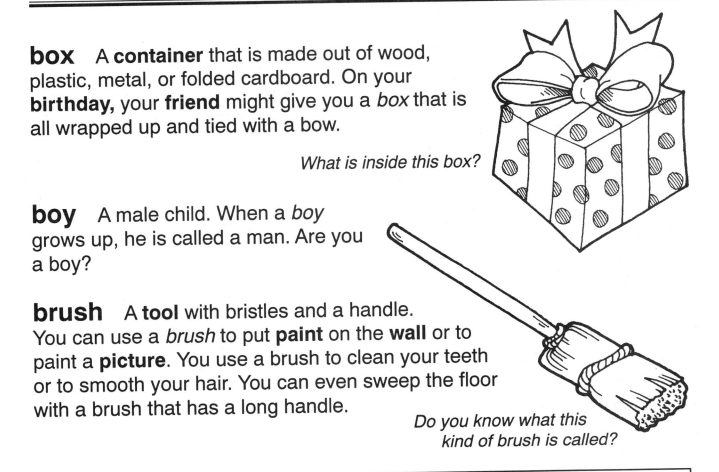

*How are a **bowl**, a **bottle**, and a **box** alike?*
How are they different?
*Look up **bottle, bowl,** and **box** to help you decide!*

bus A large **vehicle** that can carry lots of people. Many children ride a *bus* when they go to **school**. Other people ride a bus to work. When you go to school, will you ride on a bus with your **friends**?

butterfly A beautiful **insect** that can fly. A *butterfly* has a thin **body** and four colorful wings. Butterflies fly only in the daytime. What do you think they do at **night**?

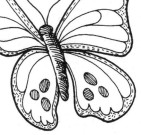

cake A sweet **food** that is eaten after lunch or dinner, or for a snack. Most *cakes* are made from flour, **eggs,** butter, and sugar. On your **birthday,** you might have a cake with candles on it. How many candles will you count on your next birthday cake?

car A **vehicle** with four **wheels** that carries people along a **road** from place to place. The driver of a *car* has to watch the road very carefully and not get in the way of other cars.

How many doors does this car have?

cat A small, furry **animal** with four legs, soft paws, and whiskers. Some *cats* are small and live in **houses** as **pets**. These pet cats can purr and meow. A purr is a soft sound they make when they are happy. A meow is a little sound pet cats make when they want to tell you something. Other cats are big and wild and live in the woods or in the **jungle**. These wild cats don't meow—they roar!

chair A piece of furniture that you can sit on. Most *chairs* have four legs and a back you can lean against. Do you have a special chair at home?

cheese A **food** that is made from **milk**. Most *cheese* is either orange, yellow, or white. Some cheese has holes. You can slice cheese and put it between pieces of bread to make a sandwich. You can melt cheese and put it on all kinds of foods.

chicken An **animal** that lives on a **farm**. Female *chickens,* called hens, are **birds** that lay **eggs**. They sit on the eggs and keep them warm until the baby chickens are born. Both chickens and eggs are good to eat. Chickens can fly, but not very high.

circle A shape that does not have any **corners**. A *circle* is round. You can use a circle to draw a ball or a **clock**. What else can you draw with a circle?

*Does this little **cat** do something that this big cat does not do?*
*Look up **cat** to find out.*
*Would you want a **lion** to live in your home?*
*Look up **lion** to be sure!*

Look at the words and pictures on the page. Can you find some more items in this dictionary that belong here? Add more words and pictures in the space below.

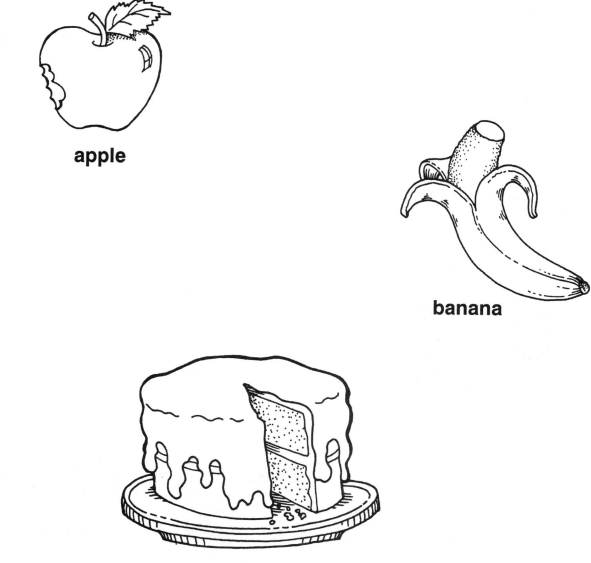

apple

banana

cake

Why do these items belong together? Write your answer on the lines.

_____

_____

_____

Look at the words and pictures on the page. Can you find some more items in this dictionary that belong here? Add more words and pictures in the space below.

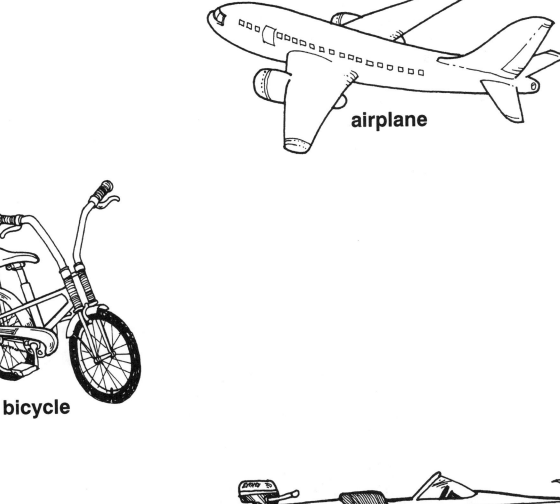

airplane

bicycle

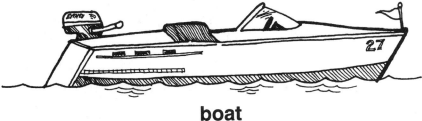

boat

Why do these items belong together? Write your answer on the lines.

_____

_____

_____

clock   A **machine** that tells you what time it is. Some *clocks* have hands that tell the time of day or **night**. Other clocks have **numbers** that show the time. Do you know how to tell time?

What time is it on this clock?

coat   A piece of clothing that keeps you warm. You wear a *coat* over your other clothes when it is cold outside or when it is raining.

coin   A piece of **money** that is made out of metal. **Pennies, nickels, dimes,** and **quarters** are all *coins*. Which coin would you like to have more of? Look up **penny, nickel, dime,** and **quarter** to see!

container   A **jar,** can, **bowl,** or **box** that holds something. *Containers* can hold wet or dry things like **juice** or **food.** Can you name another container that you use?

cookie   A small, flat **cake** that is sweet and good to eat. *Cookies* are fun to eat after lunch or dinner or for a snack. But don't eat too many—you might get a stomachache!

What kind of cookie is this?

corner   The place where two sides come together. A **triangle** has three *corners* and a **square** has four. The corner of a room is where two **walls** come together. What happens at the corner of a street?

cow A large **animal** that lives on a **farm**. *Cows* have four legs, small ears, and two big, friendly eyes. The **milk** that you drink comes from a cow. A baby cow is called a calf.

crab An **animal** that lives in or near the **water**. A *crab* walks sideways on eight legs. A crab has two large claws that it uses to protect itself. Watch out!

cup A small **container** that can hold one helping of **liquid** for you to drink. You can drink **milk** or **juice** from a *cup*. Some cups have a handle, but some do not. Do you have a favorite cup?

*How are a **crab** and a **spider** alike?*
How are they different?
*Look up **crab** and look up **spider** to help you find out!*

What coins could you use to buy the toy? How many different combinations of coins could you use? Which combination uses the fewest coins?

Finish the labels for the picture below. The first letter of each label is given as a clue. If you are not sure, use the letter given to help you look up the word in this dictionary.

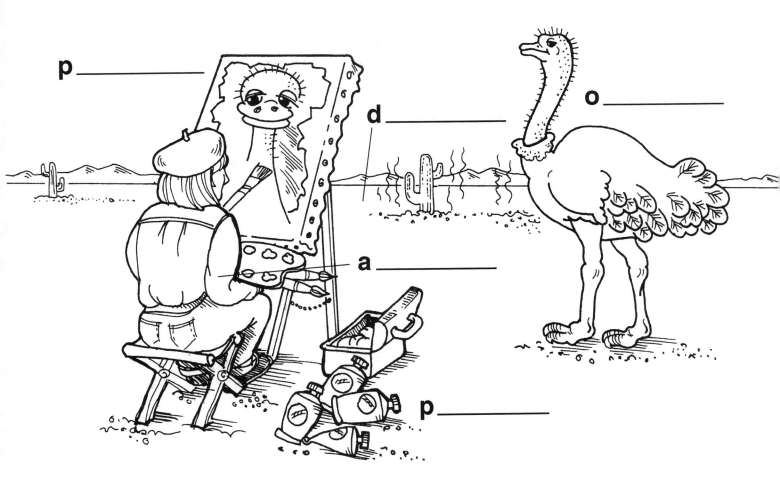

p_____

d_____

o_____

a_____

p_____

desert   A hot, dry place that is covered with sand. Very little **rain** falls on the *desert*. Cactus **plants** grow in the desert because they do not need much **water**. What else might you find in the desert?

dime   A silver-colored **coin** that is equal to ten **pennies**. A *dime* is more **money** than a penny or a **nickel,** but a **quarter** is more money than a dime.

dinosaur   An **animal** that lived millions of years ago. *Dinosaurs* came in many shapes and sizes. Some dinosaurs ate meat and others ate **plants**. Some dinosaurs were so big that the **earth** shook when they walked! No one knows exactly why the dinosaurs disappeared, but scientists are trying to find out.

dog   A furry **animal** with four legs. Most *dogs* are friendly and make good **pets**. Some dogs work. They can be used to herd **sheep,** to help blind people find their way around, or to guard buildings.

dollar   A piece of paper **money** that is equal to one hundred **pennies**. Some people would rather have a *dollar* bill because it is easy to carry. Other people would rather have all the pennies. Do you know what other coins add up to a dollar?

duck   A **bird** that lives near the **water**. *Ducks* have hard, flat bills, or mouths. Ducks have webbed feet, which makes them good swimmers. They can also walk and fly.

earth **1.** A planet in the solar system. *Earth* is the planet you live on. **2.** A piece of dry **land** or dirt. When you grow a **garden,** you put the **plants** in the *earth*.

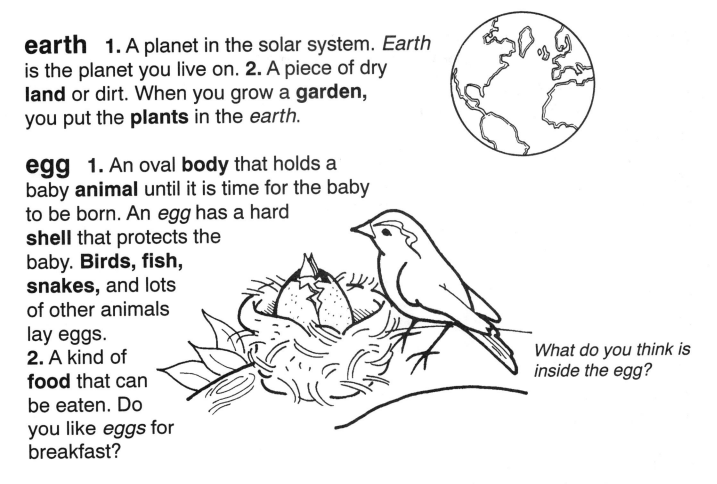

egg **1.** An oval **body** that holds a baby **animal** until it is time for the baby to be born. An *egg* has a hard **shell** that protects the baby. **Birds, fish, snakes,** and lots of other animals lay eggs. **2.** A kind of **food** that can be eaten. Do you like *eggs* for breakfast?

What do you think is inside the egg?

elephant The biggest and strongest **land animal** alive today. An *elephant* is gray and has a long nose called a trunk that it uses as a hand. Elephants like to splash themselves with mud and **water** to keep cool. Elephants have the largest ears of all the animals. Can you guess what else elephants do with their big ears besides hear?

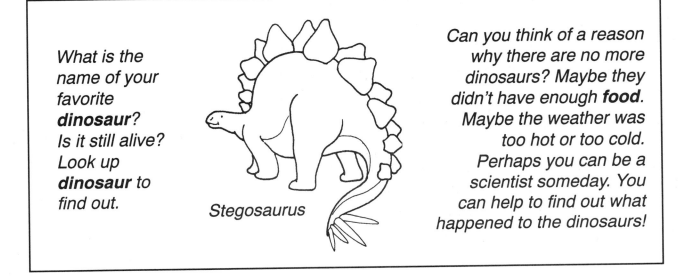

What is the name of your favorite **dinosaur**? *Is it still alive? Look up* **dinosaur** *to find out.*

Stegosaurus

Can you think of a reason why there are no more dinosaurs? Maybe they didn't have enough **food**. *Maybe the weather was too hot or too cold. Perhaps you can be a scientist someday. You can help to find out what happened to the dinosaurs!*

Change the first letter in each word to help the cat climb up the ladder! Go in order of the alphabet, creating words that make sense.

Change the last, first, or middle letter in each word to help the pig climb up the ladder!

cup

_ u t

b _ t

_ i t

p i _

p i g

envelope   A holder that is made out of folded paper. An *envelope* is a lot like a **pocket**. When you write a **letter,** you slip it into an envelope. Always remember to put a stamp on your envelope before you mail it.

eraser   A **school tool** that is used to wipe away **pencil** marks that you do not want. If you make a mistake with your pencil, don't get upset. Just use your *eraser* to wipe the mistake away!

farm   A piece of **land** where people grow **food** and keep **animals**. A **chicken** and a **cow** are both *farm* animals. Can you name any more? Carrots and lettuce can be grown on a farm. Do you know what the person who takes care of a farm is called?

What kind of food is growing on this farm?

fish   An **animal** that lives in the **water**. Most *fish* are covered with thin, bony scales that protect them. A fish uses its fins, which are like arms, and its tail to swim. Fish breathe through holes in their sides that are called gills.

flag   A piece of cloth that is decorated with special colors and **pictures**. Each color or picture has its own special meaning. Every country has its own *flag.* What country do you live in? What colors are in your country's flag?

flower   A beautiful part of a **plant**. Many *flowers* have sweet smells and bright colors. Flowers can be planted in a **garden**. They can also be put in a vase indoors. Some flowers grow wild outside.

What are these flowers called?

food   The name given to anything you eat. All **animals** and **plants** need *food* to grow and live. Do you need food? Do you need anything else to live?

Can you name this food?

forest   A place where many **trees** and **plants** grow and cover the **land**. The *forest* is a home for lots of wild **animals,** such as foxes and squirrels. Can you name another animal that lives in the forest?

fork   An eating **tool**. Most *forks* are made out of metal and have three or four sharp points. You use a fork to pick up **food**. What else can you use to pick up food?

*How is each **animal** alike?*
There is something that they all like to do.
*Look up **elephant, pig,** and **rhinoceros** to help you decide!*

Complete this picture. On the lines below, write a story to go with your completed drawing. Be sure to include the words **rhinoceros** and **pajamas** in your story.

_____

_____

_____

_____

_____

_____

_____

_____

Make a single word into a poem! Across each letter of the word, write another word that somehow relates. Look at the example. Try to make one up yourself!

s l e d
f u **n**
c **o** l d
w i n t e r

g
a
r
d
e
n

friend   A person you like. A *friend* is also a person who likes you. It is fun to play and spend time with your friends.

frog   A small **animal** that lives in or near the **water**. A *frog* has webbed feet and strong back legs that it uses to swim and jump. Some frogs make a loud noise. Do you know how to make that sound?

garden   A piece of **land** where **vegetables** or **flowers** are planted. The **plants** in a *garden* need **water** and **food** so they can grow, just like you do! Where does the water for a garden come from?

giraffe   A wild **animal** that has a very long neck. The *giraffe* is the tallest animal in the world. A grown-up giraffe can be six times taller than you are! Giraffes live in grassy areas and eat the leaves off the tops of the **trees**.

girl   A female child. When a *girl* grows up, she is called a woman. Are you a girl?

glass   **1.** A hard material that you can see through. Is *glass* like a **window**? Look up **window** to see! **2.** A **container** that you can drink from. A *glass* is like a **cup** without a handle.

glove   A piece of clothing that you wear over your hands to keep them warm or dry. A *glove* has a place for each finger on your hand. Sometimes gloves are worn to protect hands from dirt, fire, or sharp objects.

grape   A small, round fruit that grows on long **plants** called vines. *Grapes* grow in large bunches. Grapes can be red, green, or purple. All grapes are delicious—and good for you, too!

grass   A green **plant** that grows in groups and covers the ground. **Cows** like to eat *grass,* and so do **horses**. A piece of grass is called a blade, because it looks sharp, like a **knife** blade.

*What kind of **animal** is resting in the grass?*

*Debbie wants to eat some **food**. What **tools** will she use to eat it?*

spoon   knife   hammer   fork

Look up the words above to help you find out!
*The **dog** wants to eat some food. What will she use?*

Use this dictionary to find some animals that belong in each category below.
Write their names on the lines.

two legs	four legs	more legs
KANGROO		

How many animals did you find for each category? Which category has the
most animals?

Use this dictionary to find some animals that belong in each category below. Write their names on the lines.

live in water

_____

_____

_____

_____

_____

live on land

_____

_____

_____

_____

_____

How many animals did you find for each category? Did you find any animals that belong in both categories?

hammer A **tool** with a handle and a heavy head. The head of a *hammer* is used to hit nails into wood.

hat A piece of clothing that you wear on your head. You can wear a *hat* to cover your head in the **rain,** in the **sun,** and in the **snow**. Some people wear hats just because they like them!

helicopter A **vehicle** that flies. *Helicopters* are different from **airplanes** because they can fly in any direction. Helicopters fly forward and backward. They can even fly straight up in the air and stop moving!

hippopotamus A large **animal** that lives in or near the **water**. A *hippopotamus,* or hippo, has a heavy, round-shaped **body** and thick skin. Hippopotamuses have small eyes and ears on their large heads, but their mouths are really big!

horse A large **farm animal**. A *horse* has a long tail that it uses to swish away flies. A horse also has a long mane on its back that is like your hair. Horses can run very fast on their four long legs. Some horses will let you sit on their backs and go for a ride.

house A building where people live. *Houses* come in all shapes, sizes, and colors. A house has different rooms where people eat, sleep, wash, work, or relax. Do you know the **names** of any of these rooms? Maybe one of them is yours!

ice Frozen, hard **water**. You can put pieces, or cubes, of *ice* in a **glass** to keep a drink cold. You can skate on ice when a **lake** or a pond freezes in the winter.

ice cream A cold, sweet **food** that is made from cream and **water**. Sometimes *ice cream* has fruit, nuts, or chocolate sauce already mixed in. You can put ice cream in a dish and eat it with a **spoon,** or you can put it in a cone and lick it!

insect A small **animal** with six legs. Some *insects* crawl, and other insects have wings and can fly. Some insects bite, so be careful! Others, like ladybugs, are very friendly.

Do you know what these insects are called?

*How are a **glove** and a **mitten** alike?*
How are they different?
*Look up **glove** and **mitten** to help you find out.*
*Now look up **sock**. Is a sock more like a glove or a mitten?*

Look at the words and pictures on the page. Can you find some more items in this dictionary that belong here? Add more words and pictures in the space below.

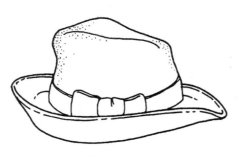

hat

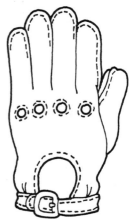

glove

coat

Why do these items belong together? Write your answer on the lines.

_____

_____

_____

Make a single word into a poem! Across each letter of the word, write another word that somehow relates. You can turn back to page 25 to see how this is done.

h
o
r
s
e

Draw a picture to go with your poem.

iron An electric **tool** that gets hot when you turn it on. An *iron* is used to smooth the wrinkles out of clothes.

island A piece of **land** that has **water** all around it. Have you ever been to an *island*? How would you get across the water to an island?

jacket A piece of clothing that you wear over your other clothes when it is cool outside. A *jacket* will keep you warm, but it is not as long as a **coat**. Wear a coat when it is cold. Wear a jacket when it is cool.

Do you know how to open this jacket?

jar A **glass container** that has a wide opening at the top and a lid that screws on or off. Pickles come in a *jar*. So does **jelly**. What other things come in a jar?

What do you think is inside this jar?

jelly A soft **food** that is mostly made from fruit and sugar. You can spread *jelly* on bread or toast to make a sandwich. Some people like to eat jelly with peanut butter. Do you?

job The work that a person or thing does. The *job* of a mail carrier is to deliver the mail. The job of a fire fighter is to put out fires. What is the job of a **car**? Most people get paid **money** to do their jobs. What kind of job would you like to do when you are older?

juice A drink that is made from fruits or **vegetables**. *Juice* is delicious—and good for you, too! What kind of juice do you like best?

What kind of juice is this?

jungle A warm, often wet outdoor place that has many **trees** and bushes. *Jungles* are the homes of lots of **animals** and **plants**. Monkeys swing from the trees in the jungle. Can you think of another animal that lives in the jungle?

kangaroo An **animal** with strong back legs for jumping and a long tail. A mother *kangaroo* carries her baby in a pouch on her stomach. A baby kangaroo is called a joey.

*Is a **spider** an **animal**?*
*Is an **insect** an animal?*
Is a spider an insect?
*Look up **animal**. Look up **spider**. Look up **insect**.*
You decide!

Complete this picture. On the lines below, write a story to go with your completed drawing. Be sure to include the words **worm** and **banana** in your story.

_____

_____

_____

_____

_____

_____

_____

_____

_____

_____

Finish the labels for the picture below. The first letter of each label is given as a clue. If you are not sure, use the letter given to help you look up the word in this dictionary.

r _____

l _____   o _____

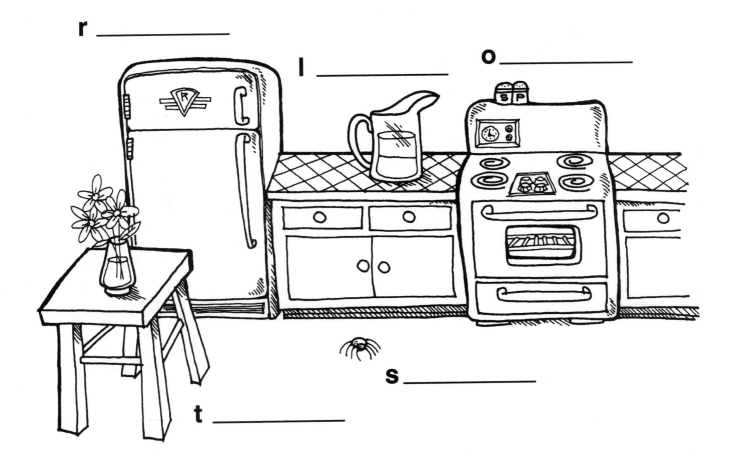

s _____

t _____

key   A small metal **tool** that is used to open and close a lock. After you lock the door to your home, you need a *key* to open the door.

kitten   A baby **cat**. When a *kitten* is born, the mother cat takes care of it and feeds it **milk** from her **body**. Kittens are very cuddly and playful.

knife   A **tool** that has a handle and a sharp blade. You can use a *knife* to cut all kinds of **foods,** like bread, meat, and **vegetables**.

ladder   A set of steps that you can sometimes move from one place to another. You can climb a *ladder* to reach high places. Or you can climb a ladder at the playground to go down the slide.

What happens if you climb up this ladder and go down the slide?

lake   A large area of **water** with **land** all around it. *Lakes* are sometimes filled with **fish** and **plants**. There are lots of things to do on a lake. Can you name some of them?

land   Any part of the planet **Earth** that is not covered by **water**. You can stand on *land,* but you cannot stand on water.

leaf A thin, flat green part of a **tree** or **plant** that grows on a branch. A *leaf* can become red, yellow, or brown in the fall. Some trees lose their leaves in the winter. Some **vegetable** leaves, like spinach, are good to eat.

letter **1.** A message that is written on paper. You can put a *letter* in an **envelope** that has a stamp on it and mail it. **2.** One part of the **alphabet**. Can you remember how many *letters* there are in the alphabet?

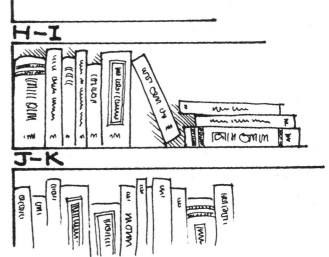

library A room or building where **books** are kept. You can borrow books from a **school** or town *library* to take home and read. You can enjoy and learn a lot from library books.

What is your favorite library book?

mountain

island

*How are a **mountain** and an **island** the same? How are they different? Look up **island** and look up **mountain** to help you decide!*

If you could have any animal in the world for a pet, which one would you choose? Use the questions below to help you write about your perfect pet. Draw a picture of your pet in the box.

What animal would you choose?_____

Why? _____

_____

What would you name your pet? _____

What would your pet need to stay happy and healthy?_____

_____

_____

My Perfect Pet

Finish the labels for the shapes below. The first letter of each shape's name is given as a clue. If you are not sure, use the letter given to help you look up the word in this dictionary.

c _____

r _____

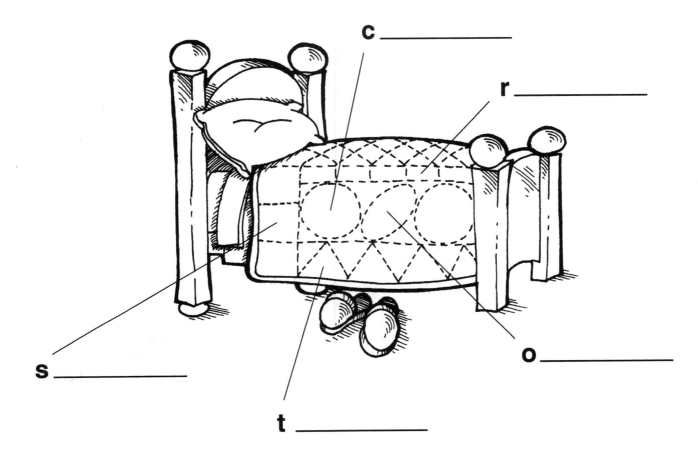

s _____

o _____

t _____

Do you know the names of any other shapes? Write them on the lines.

_____   _____   _____

light Something that helps you see in the dark. In the day, the **sun** makes *light* that helps you to see. At **night,** you can turn on a light in your bedroom.

lion A big, wild **cat** that lives near the **jungle**. A male *lion* has a furry collar of hair around its neck called a mane. Lions roar when they speak. Do you know what a baby lion is called?

liquid Something that is wet. A *liquid* is not hard or full of air. **Water, milk,** and **juice** are all *liquids*. Can you name something else that is a liquid?

*What kind of liquid is in the **glass**?*

machine Something that does a special **job**. A *machine* has lots of moving pieces that work together. A **car** and an **airplane** are machines. Is a **bicycle** a machine?

map A special kind of **picture** that shows where places are. On a *map,* you could see the **Earth,** a country, or a city. When you are lost, a map can help you find your way.

What country is shown on the map?

medicine Something that helps you get well when you are sick. If you are sick, the doctor may give you *medicine* to help you feel better.

milk A white **liquid** that comes from **cows**. You can put *milk* on cereal, or you can just drink it by itself. Milk is very good for you and helps to keep your bones and teeth strong.

mirror A smooth piece of **glass** that shows a **picture** of things in front of it. When you look in a *mirror,* you can see yourself! What you see in a mirror is called a reflection.

mitten A piece of clothing that you wear over your hand. A *mitten* has one small place for your thumb and one big place for your other four fingers. You can wear mittens to keep your hands warm.

*How many **letters** do you see in this **picture**?*
*Look up **letter** to help you decide!*

Use the map to find the treasure! Before you begin, make a prediction. Where do you think the treasure is located?

Begin at the space marked START. Go four spaces north. Go three spaces east. Go two spaces north. Go four spaces west. Go two spaces south. Place an X on this spot. Draw a picture of the treasure you see there.

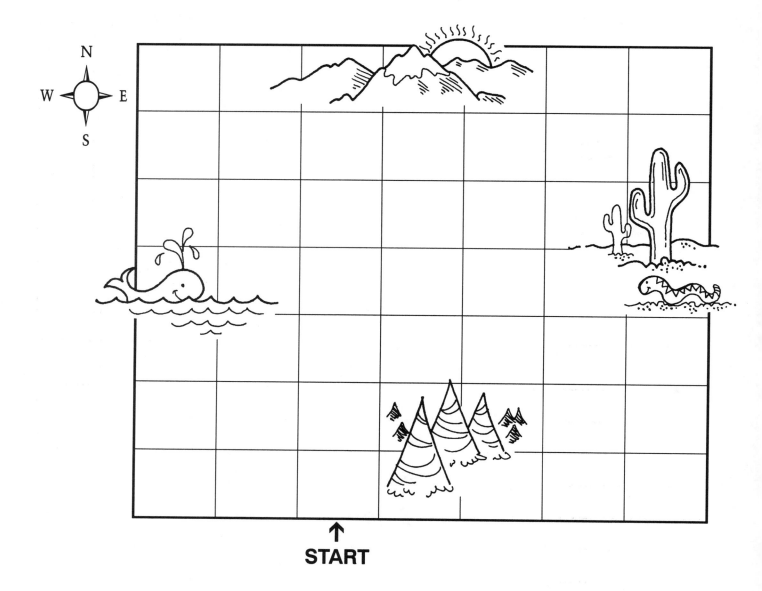

Is the treasure in the ocean, the mountains, the forest, or the desert? Was your prediction correct?

Complete this picture. On the lines below, write a story to go with your completed drawing. Be sure to include the words **moon** and **mirror** in your story.

_____

_____

_____

_____

_____

_____

_____

_____

_____

_____

money What we use to buy things. Some *money* is made out of paper, and some is made out of metal. **Coins** are money made out of metal.

How much money do you see?

moon The **Earth**'s nearest neighbor in space. At **night** you can sometimes see the *moon* shining brightly in the sky. When the moon is full, it looks like a **circle**. But sometimes the moon is shaped like a **banana**.

Is the moon full?

mountain A piece of **land** that is much higher than the land around it. Sometimes the tops of *mountains* are covered with **snow**. A mountain can even have **water** all around it, with only the top showing!

name A word that is used to call a person, place, or thing. Almost everything has a *name*. You have a name. The **book** you are reading has a name. What is it called?

Can you guess the name of this book?

nest A home that **animals** make to hold their babies. **Birds** use sticks, leaves, and dried **grass** to make their *nests*. What other things can birds use when they are building their nests?

nickel A silver-colored **coin** that is equal to five **pennies**. A *nickel* is more **money** than a penny. But a **dime** and a **quarter** are both more money than a nickel!

night The part of the day when it is dark. The *night* starts when the **sun** sets at the end of the day. The night ends when the sun comes up in the morning. What do people do at night?

number Something to count with that tells you how many. 5, 10, and 20 are all *numbers*. Is E a number? If you have candles on your **birthday cake,** you can count them and give them a number.

What is the number of candles on this cake?

ocean A very large **body** of **water**. *Ocean* water is salty. Many kinds of **plants** and **animals** live in the ocean. Do you know the **names** of any of them?

What animal can you see in the ocean?

*Which **picture** shows a **mirror**?*
*Which picture shows a **window**?*
*Look up **mirror** and **window** to help you decide!*

What is the best birthday celebration you can think of? Plan a party for yourself or someone else. Use the questions below to help you. Write your ideas on the lines. Draw a picture of your super celebration in the box.

Who is the party for? _____

Where will the party be? _____

When will it take place? _____

_____

What will you do? _____

_____

What do you need? _____

_____

HAPPY BIRTHDAY! HAPPY BIRTHDAY! HAPPY BIRTHDAY! HAPPY BIRTHDAY!

HAPPY BIRTHDAY! HAPPY BIRTHDAY! HAPPY BIRTHDAY!

HAPPY BIRTHDAY! HAPPY BIRTHDAY!

HAPPY BIRTHDAY! HAPPY BIRTHDAY! HAPPY BIRTHDAY! HAPPY BIRTHDAY!

Here is a chart of the numbers from 1 to 50. Find the secret number!
This number is greater than 10. It is less than 30. You can reach it when
counting by fives, but not when counting by tens. It has a 2 in the tens
place. What is the number?

1	2	3	4	5	6	7	8	9	10
11	12	13	14	15	16	17	18	19	20
21	22	23	24	25	26	27	28	29	30
31	32	33	34	35	36	37	38	39	40
41	42	43	44	45	46	47	48	49	50

The secret number is 25!

octopus An **animal** that lives in the **ocean**. An *octopus* has a soft **body** and eight long arms. When an octopus is afraid, it squirts blue ink into the ocean to hide from its enemies.

orange A round, juicy fruit that grows on a **tree**. The inside of an *orange* is the color orange. Do you think that is why it is called an orange?

ostrich The largest **bird** in the world. An *ostrich* has two long legs, a long neck, and long, beautiful feathers. Ostriches are so big and heavy that they cannot fly—but they can run very fast!

oval A shape. An *oval* looks like a **circle** that somebody stepped on. Most **eggs** are shaped like an oval. You can use an oval to draw a melon.

What else can you draw with an oval shape?

oven A kitchen **machine** that gets very hot and is used to cook **food**. You can cook a turkey or bake **cookies** in an *oven*. What else can you make in an oven?

paint A wet material that is used to color things. You can use a paintbrush to put *paint* on the **wall** or to make a **picture**. But the paint does not stay wet. It dries after a while. When you see a **sign** that says WET PAINT, watch out!

pajamas Clothes that you wear when you are in **bed**. When it is time to go to sleep at **night,** you put on your *pajamas*. What else should you do?

pants Clothing that you wear over your hips and legs. Some *pants* are closed with a **zipper**. Other pants are closed with buttons.

parade A special outdoor show where people march down the street. In a *parade,* people sometimes wear costumes, ride **horses,** or hold big balloons. What are some of the days on which you can see a parade?

*How are these **animals** alike?*
How are they different?
*Look up **spider** and **octopus** to help you find out!*
An octopus squirts ink at its enemies.
What does a spider do to its enemies?

Number the pictures in the order you think they might happen. Put a number from 1 to 5 on the lines below them.

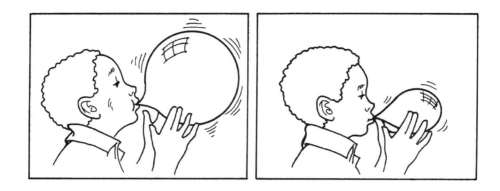

_____   _____

_____   _____   _____

On the lines below, write a story to go with the pictures.

_____

_____

_____

_____

_____

_____

_____

_____

Draw a hippopotamus in the large box.
Use the sample pictures to help you.
Write a story about your hippo on the
lines below it.

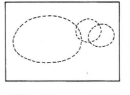

pen A writing **tool** that is full of ink. A *pen* can be used for writing **letters** on paper. Most grown-ups use pens at work to sign their **name** on letters. It is best to use a pen to write when you will not want to erase anything.

pencil A writing **tool** that has a sharp point at one end and an **eraser** at the other end. If you make a mark with a *pencil,* you can erase it if you want to. How is a pencil different from a **pen**?

penny A **coin** that is made out of a brown metal called copper. A *penny* is equal to one cent. A penny is less **money** than a **nickel,** a **dime,** or a **quarter**.

pet An **animal** that a person keeps and takes care of. *Pets* have to be given **food, water,** and lots of love. **Cats** and **dogs** make great pets. What other animals are good pets?

picture A drawing or a photograph of a person or a thing. You can draw or paint a *picture.* You can also take a picture with a camera.

What do you think this is a picture of?

pie A sweet **food** that is round and is filled with good things to eat. Some *pies* have a crust with fruit inside. Other pies can be made from chocolate and cream.

What shape is made when you cut a pie?

pig A **farm animal** with four legs, a flat nose, and a curly tail. *Pigs* are smart. They like to lie in mud to stay cool. What do you do to stay cool?

plant Any living thing that is not an **animal**. A *plant* cannot move from place to place, and it cannot see, hear, smell, or touch. Some plants live in the dirt and some live in the **water**. A **tree,** a **flower, grass,** and seaweed are all plants.

You can smell this plant. Can it smell you?

plate A flat **container** that holds **food**. Most *plates* are round, but some are **oval** shaped. When you set the **table,** you put one plate out for each person who will eat. What else can you give each person besides a plate?

*Which **pictures** go together?*
*Look up **paint, spoon,** and **hammer** to help you decide!*

Number the pictures in the order you think they might happen. Put a number from 1 to 5 on the lines below them.

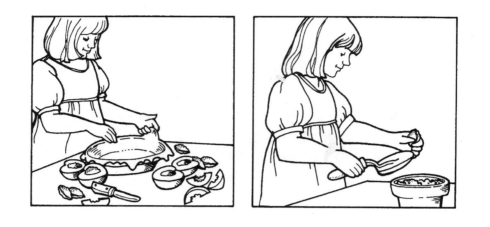

_____   _____

_____   _____   _____

On the lines below, write a story to go with the pictures.

_____

_____

_____

_____

_____

_____

_____

_____

Draw a frog in the large box. Use the sample pictures to help you. Write a story about your frog on the lines below it.

pocket   A piece of cloth that is sewn around three sides onto clothes. People can keep special things in their *pockets*!

What do you think is in this pocket?

pot   A deep, round **container**. Some *pots* are used for cooking. Other pots are used for planting **flowers**. What kinds of pots do you have in your home?

potato   A **vegetable** that grows under the ground. A *potato* is good to eat—and good for you, too! There are lots of ways to cook a potato. Potatoes can be boiled in a **pot,** baked in an **oven,** or fried in a pan.

What kind of potato is this?

puppy   A baby **dog**. When a *puppy* is born, the mother dog takes care of it and feeds it **milk** from her **body**. Puppies are very cute and playful.

quarter   A silver-colored **coin** that is equal to twenty-five pennies. A *quarter* is worth more than the sum of a **penny,** a **nickel,** and a **dime**!

question   Words you say or write when you want to know something. If you ask a *question,* another person might tell you the answer. There are lots of questions in this **book**. Can you answer any of them?

quilt A **bed** covering made out of pieces of cloth that are sewn together. *Quilts* are stuffed with soft material. Some quilts have a lot of colors. Some quilts show a **picture**. Do you have a quilt on your bed?

rabbit A small, gentle **animal**. A *rabbit* has long ears and a round, fluffy tail. Rabbits use their strong back legs to hop and run. Some rabbits are wild and live in the woods. Other rabbits are kept as **pets**.

*What **name** would you give this rabbit?*

radio A **machine** that is used to send messages, music, or other sounds. When you turn on a *radio,* sometimes you can hear a person talking. Sometimes you can hear people playing music. But you can never see the people making the sounds on a radio.

*What is the same about an **envelope,** a **pocket,** and a **pot**?*
*Look up **envelope, pocket,** and **pot** to help you find out!*

Which of these words can go in a pocket? Which can go in a pot?
Which can go in an envelope?

coin **potato** **plant** **letter**

Look up each word to help you decide!

What else can go in a pocket?
What else can go in a pot?

Bicycles are lots of fun, but can you design a better bicycle? Will it have a rocket engine or a radio? Will it float or fly? Give it a try! Use the questions below to help you. Draw a picture of your super bicycle in the box.

What can your bike do that other bikes cannot do? _____

_____

What materials do you need to build this bike? _____

_____

Why do you think this bike is better than others? _____

_____

_____

My Super Bicycle

Number the pictures in the order you think they might happen. Put a
number from 1 to 5 on the lines below them.

———

———   ———   ———

On the lines below, write a story to go with the pictures.

_____

_____

_____

_____

_____

_____

_____

rain   **Water** that drops down from the clouds. **Plants** use the *rain* to grow. People and **animals** use the rain for drinking **water**. When it rains, you can carry an **umbrella** to stay dry. What clothes can you wear in the rain?

rainbow   A beautiful band of colored **light** that is sometimes seen in the sky after it rains. The light from the **sun** comes through the tiny drops of **rain** in the sky and makes a *rainbow*.

What colors are in this rainbow?

raincoat   A **coat** that is worn in the **rain**. Some *raincoats* are made out of cloth and some are made out of a shiny material called plastic. When it rains, you can wear a raincoat to stay dry.

rectangle   A shape that has four sides and four **corners**. You can use a *rectangle* to draw a **table** or a door.

What else can you draw with a rectangle shape?

refrigerator   A **machine** that is used to keep **food** cold. You keep **milk** and **eggs** in the *refrigerator* to stop them from spoiling.

What other kinds of foods can you see?

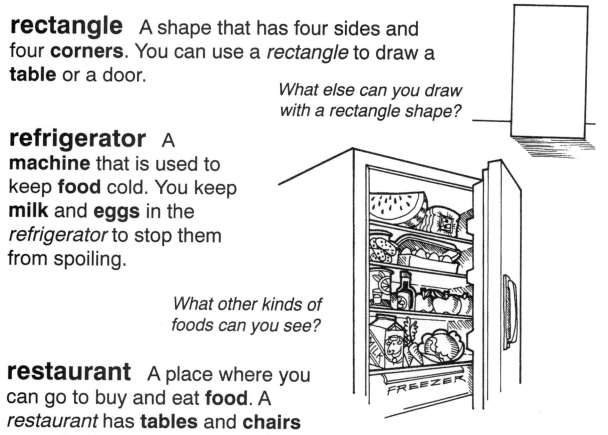

restaurant   A place where you can go to buy and eat **food**. A *restaurant* has **tables** and **chairs** and a large kitchen. People eat at a restaurant when they are away from home or if they don't want to make their own food.

rhinoceros A large wild **animal** that has thick, wrinkled skin and one or two pointed horns that stick up from its nose. A *rhinoceros* is quiet and harmless unless it is hurt or confused. Rhinoceroses are very big and like to lie in mud to keep cool. Do you like to lie in mud?

road A cleared path that is used to go from place to place. You can drive a **car** or a **truck** on a *road*. You can walk at the side of a road. Some roads are bumpy and made of dirt. Other roads are smoothed with a dark, sticky material called tar.

roof The top covering for a **house** or a building. When it rains, the people inside the house or building do not get wet. The *roof* keeps the **rain** out.

Look at the lists of words below.
*Which are you most likely to find at a **restaurant**?*

quarter
dog
people
dinosaur

egg
potato
garden
table

Complete this picture. On the lines below, write a story to go with your completed drawing. Be sure to include the words **vacuum** and **roof** in your story.

Make a single word into a poem! Across each letter of the word, write another word that somehow relates. You can turn back to page 25 to see how this is done.

b
i
r
d

Draw a picture to go with your poem.

rug   A soft covering for the floor. Some *rugs* are large enough to cover the whole floor. Other rugs are small and can go next to a **bed** or in the bathroom. What kind of a rug do you have?

ruler   A **tool** that has a straight edge and **numbers**. You can draw a straight line with a *ruler*. You can use the numbers on the ruler to tell how long the line is. Can you use a ruler to tell how long this page is?

scale   A **machine** that is used to weigh people or things. If you stand on a *scale,* the **numbers** on it will tell you how much you weigh. Try it! As you get bigger, what will happen when you stand on a scale?

school   A place where people go to learn. When you go to *school,* teachers can help you learn to use words and **numbers**. At school, you can even learn how to make music or paint a special **picture**.

season   A time of the year. There are four *seasons*—spring, summer, fall, and winter. In many places, it is hot in the summer and cold in the winter. **Flowers** grow in the spring. Leaves fall from the **trees** in the fall. Maybe that is why the season is called fall!

seed   A small part of a **flower** or a **plant** that can grow into a new plant when placed in **earth**. What will grow if you plant a carrot *seed*? What will grow if you plant an **apple** seed?

What will grow from these seeds?

sheep A shy **farm animal** that is covered with curly wool. The farmer gently cuts the wool off the *sheep*. The wool is then used to make clothes. You may have a sweater made out of wool from sheep.

shell A hard covering that some **animals** have. *Shells* protect the animals or their babies. Snails, turtles, and **crabs** all have shells. So do baby **birds,** which are born in **eggs**. Do you have a shell?

What is inside this shell?

shirt A piece of clothing that you can wear over the top of your **body**. Some *shirts* have short sleeves and some have long sleeves. Some shirts have buttons and others do not. A shirt with short sleeves and no buttons is called a T-shirt.

*What would you put in each **container**?*

Draw a sheep in the large box. Use the sample pictures to help you. Write a story about your sheep on the lines below it.

Make a single word into a poem! Across each letter of the word, write another word that somehow relates. You can turn back to page 25 to see how this is done.

t
i
g
e
r

Draw a picture to go with your poem.

shoe A covering that you can wear on your foot. *Shoes* come in sets of two because people have two feet. The two shoes look alike, but they are not exactly the same. One shoe is made to fit the shape of your right foot. The other shoe is made to fit the shape of your left foot.

Which foot will this shoe fit?

sign A piece of paper, wood, or metal that has words that tell a message. A *sign* can tell you where you are or where you are going. Other signs tell you what to do or warn you of danger.

sink A **container** found in the kitchen or in the bathroom that can hold **water**. You can wash your hands and brush your teeth in the bathroom *sink*. In which sink do people wash dishes?

skirt A piece of clothing that hangs from the waist. A *skirt* does not have legs like **pants** do. A skirt is open at the bottom.

snake An **animal** that has a long **body** and no legs, arms, or wings. A *snake* has to crawl or creep along the ground by moving its body in and out. Be careful if you ever see a snake. Some of them can hurt you!

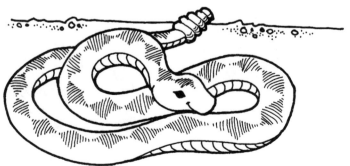

snow Tiny white pieces of frozen **water**. *Snow* falls to the ground from the clouds when it is very cold outside. What other kind of water falls from the clouds? You can ride on a sled and play games in snow!

sock A soft piece of clothing that you wear on your foot. *Socks* come in sets of two because people have two feet. You have to put on your socks before you put on your **shoes**!

spider A small **animal** that crawls on eight legs. Most *spiders* spin sticky webs to catch **insects** for **food**. A spider's web can be very pretty to look at, but it is dangerous for insects!

Do you know a story or a song about a spider?

spoon A small **tool** that is used for eating. Most *spoons* are made out of metal and have a round shape at the end. When you eat, you can use a spoon to scoop up **food**. Do you use a spoon or a **knife** to cut meat?

*Look at these four **signs**.*
What does each one tell you?
*Look up **sign** if you need help to decide.*

Find the letter that is missing from each sequence of letters. Use the letters to spell out a secret message! Write the missing letters on the matching numbered lines below.

1. **GHIJL**
2. **UVWXZ**
3. **MOPQR**
4. **HJKLM**
5. **LNOPQ**
6. **STUVX**

7. **BDEFG**
8. **YZBCD**
9. **RTUVW**
10. **KLMNP**
11. **ACDEF**

$\overline{}$ $\overline{}$ $\overline{}$ $\overline{}$ $\overline{}$
 4   1   3   10   6

$\overline{}$ $\overline{}$ $\overline{}$ $\overline{}$ $\overline{}$ $\overline{}$!
 5   2   8   11   7   9

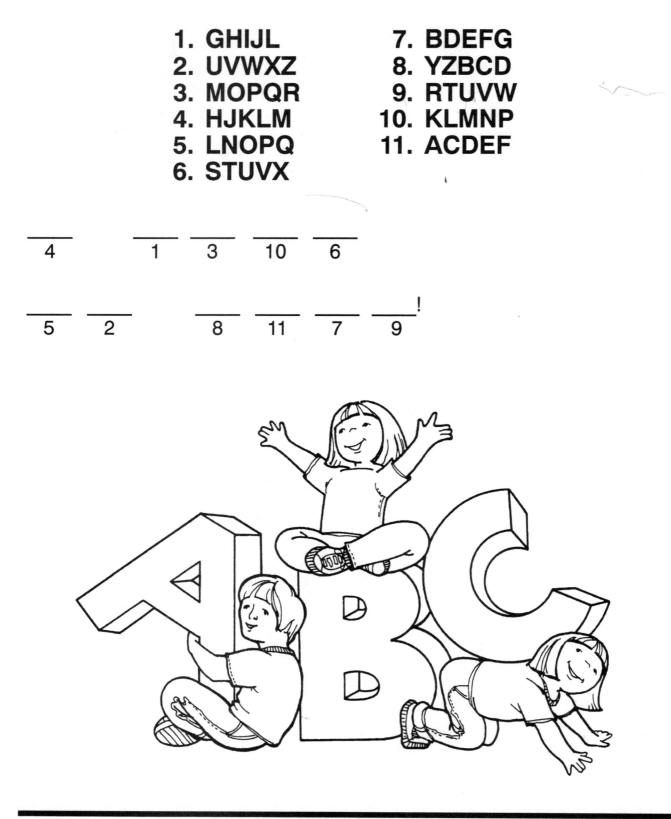

Look at the words and pictures on the page. Can you find some more items in this dictionary that belong here? Add more words and pictures in the space below.

eraser

key

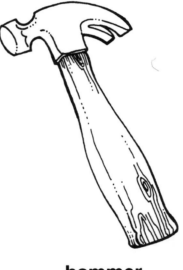

hammer

Why do these items belong together? Write your answer on the lines.

_____

_____

_____

square A shape with four sides and four **corners**. All four sides of a *square* are exactly the same length. You can use a square to draw a **window** or a **box**.

What else can you draw with a square shape?

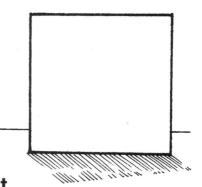

star A burning object that shines in the sky at **night**. Some *stars* look very small because they are very far away. But all stars are very, very big. The **sun** is the closest star to the **Earth**.

story Words that tell a tale. You can read a *story,* you can say a story, or you can write a story. Some stories are long and others are short. Some stories tell about true things and others tell about make-believe things. Can you make up a story of your own?

sun A **star** that shines in the sky during the day. Even though the *sun* is the closest star to the **Earth,** it is still very far away! When the sun shines, it is very hot and keeps all living things warm.

table A piece of furniture that has a flat top and some legs. When it is time to eat, you put your **plate** on a *table* and sit in a **chair**. What else can you do at a table?

telephone A **machine** that is used to talk to people. You can use the *telephone* to talk to someone who lives very far away. You can also use the telephone to talk to a **friend** who lives right next door!

Who would you like to call on this telephone?

television   A **machine** that shows a moving **picture**. Sometimes the picture tells a make-believe **story**. Sometimes the picture tells a true story or gives a message. When you watch *television,* you can hear what people are saying. You can see what people are doing.

*Is a television like a **radio**?*

tiger   A wild **animal** that lives in the **jungle**. A *tiger* is a large orange **cat** with black stripes. Tigers have sharp teeth and claws. A tiger cannot meow like a **pet** cat, but a tiger can roar like a **lion**!

tool   Something that is used to do work. A **knife** is a *tool* that is used to cut **food**. A **spoon** is a tool that is used to eat. A **pencil** is a tool that is used to write. How many more tools can you name?

sun   **star**

How are both of these words the same?
How are they different?
Only one of them shines during the day. Which one?
Don't answer too quickly.
*Look up **sun** and **star** to see if you are right!*

tooth A sharp part of an **animal**'s **body** that is used for biting and chewing. You also use your *teeth* for talking. Most animals have many teeth, but some do not even have one tooth! Do **birds** have teeth? Do **fish** have teeth?

This shark has big teeth! Is it a fish?

train A **vehicle** with **wheels** that rides on a track. A *train* has an engine that pulls it along. You can ride on a train to places that are very far away or to places that are close by. Your parents might ride the train to get to their **jobs**.

tree A tall **plant**. *Trees* have branches that stick out at their sides and roots that grow under the ground. There are many different kinds of trees. Some trees have leaves and others have needles. A tree with big branches is fun to climb!

triangle A shape that has three sides and three **corners**. You can use a *triangle* to draw a **tree**. You can use a triangle to draw the **roof** of a **house**.

What else can you draw with a triangle shape?

truck A **vehicle** with **wheels** that rides on **roads**. *Trucks* carry cargo from place to place. There are many kinds of trucks. Some trucks are open at the back. Other trucks are closed all the way around. Do you know the **names** of some different trucks?

umbrella A **tool** that keeps you dry in the **rain**. An *umbrella* has a handle to hold on to. When it rains, you can open your umbrella and hold it over your head to stay dry.

Can you use an umbrella only in the rain?

underwear Clothes that you wear under your other clothes, next to your skin. *Underwear* keeps you comfortable and warm.

What kind of underwear do you wear?

vacuum An electric **tool** that is used as a cleaner to suck up dust and dirt. You can use a *vacuum* to clean a **rug** or a floor. You can even use a vacuum with other tools to clean furniture.

vegetable A part of a **plant** that is used for **food**. Peas, **potatoes,** and carrots are all *vegetables*. Some vegetables can be eaten raw—right out of the **garden**! Other vegetables taste better when they are cooked. What kind of vegetable do you like best?

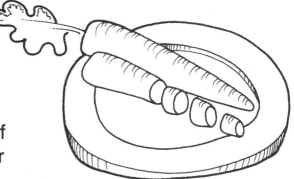

What kind of vegetable is this?

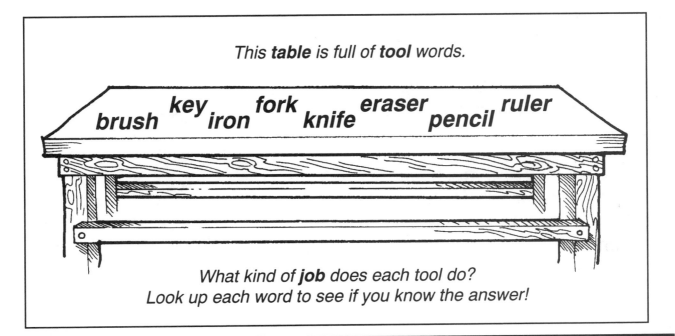

*This **table** is full of **tool** words.*

brush   key   fork   eraser   ruler
    iron   knife   pencil

*What kind of **job** does each tool do?*
Look up each word to see if you know the answer!

vehicle A **machine** that carries people or things from one place to another. **Cars** and **trucks** are *vehicles* that ride on the **road**. A **train** is a vehicle that rides on tracks. A **boat** is a vehicle that floats on the **water**. What kinds of vehicles fly in the sky?

wall The side of a building or a room. The *wall* drops from the ceiling to the floor. You can hang **pictures** on a wall. A wall can also hold back dirt or mark the edge of a piece of **land**.

How many walls do you have in your bedroom?

watch A **machine** that tells time. A *watch* is like a small **clock**. If you wear a watch strapped to your wrist, you can tell time no matter where you are!

What time is it now?

water A clear **liquid** that is good to drink. All living things need *water* to stay alive. You can also clean and cook with water. What else can you do with water?

whale A large **animal** that lives in the **ocean**. **Fish** can breathe under the **water,** but *whales* cannot. A whale must swim above the water to breathe air. The blue whale is the largest animal in the world. It is even larger than the **elephant**!

wheel Something that is shaped like a **circle** that can make **machines** roll along. A **bicycle,** a **car,** and a **truck** all have *wheels*. Do **airplanes** have wheels? Do **boats** have wheels? Think of more **vehicles** that have wheels.

window An opening in the side of a building or a **vehicle**. Most *windows* are covered by a thin piece of **glass**. A window lets you see out and lets air and **light** in. How many windows do you have in your **house**?

worm A small **animal** with a long, skinny **body** and no legs, arms, or wings. A *worm* crawls or creeps along the ground.

What other animal looks like a worm?

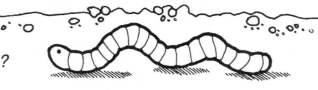

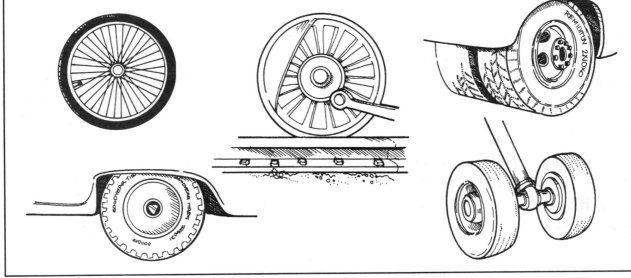

*Can you name the **vehicles** that go with these different **wheels**? You might have to look up **wheel** and **vehicle** to help you decide. On another piece of paper, draw your own **pictures** of all the vehicles and their correct wheels.*

X ray A special kind of **picture** that a doctor uses to see inside your **body**. A doctor can use the *X ray* to make sure that everything inside you is okay.

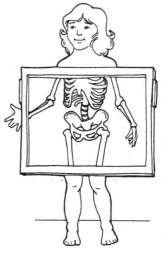

Can you name some parts of the body in this X ray?

xylophone A musical instrument. A *xylophone* has a row of wooden or metal bars that you hit with small wooden **hammers** to make music. Each bar on the xylophone makes its own sound.

yard The area around the outside of a building. A *yard* has **grass, trees,** and sometimes **flowers**. People can put up **walls** or fences to mark the edges of their yards.

yo-yo A toy that is attached to a string. When you move your hand the right way, the *yo-yo* spins up and down the string. Some people think it's hard to work a yo-yo.

zebra A wild **animal** that looks something like a **horse**. *Zebras* can run very fast on their long legs. Most zebras are white with black or brown stripes, but no two zebras look alike! Each one has different stripes.

zipper A small **machine** that is used to fasten two pieces of cloth together. A *zipper* can be opened and closed. When the zipper is open, the two pieces of cloth are not together. You probably have a zipper on your **jacket**. Do you have other clothes with a zipper?

zoo A special place where **animals** are kept so people can see them. At the *zoo,* you can see animals that come from faraway places! Many of the animals at the zoo are wild. Fences and **walls** are used to separate the animals and people and keep them all safe.